VOLUME 2

# ADVENTURES
## IN THE GOSPELS

Written by
**DAVID LUCKMAN**

Illustrated by
**SILVANA DI MARCELLO**

CF4KIDS

10 9 8 7 6 5 4 3 2 1

ISBN: 978-1-5271-1220-9

Published by Christian Focus Publications,
Geanies House, Fearn, Tain, Ross-shire, IV20 1TW, U.K.
www.christianfocus.com

Illustrations by Silvana DI Marcello
Design by Pete Barnsley (CreativeHoot.com)

Printed by Akcent Media, the Czech Republic

All words in bold are included in the glossary at the end of this book.

THIS BOOK BELONGS TO:

_____

# CONTENTS

NEW
TESTAMENT
PALESTINE

Mediterranea Sea

Phoenicia

Galilee

Tiberias
Sea of
Galilee

Nazareth

Caesarea

Decapolis

Gerasa

Samaria

Perea

Joppa

Judea

Jerusalem

Bethlehem

Philistia

Dead Sea

JERUSALEM IN
JESUS' DAY

Garden of
Gethsemane

Temple

Golgotha

Palace of
Herod
the Great

Mount of olives

# INTRODUCTION TO
# THE GOSPELS

The first four books of the New Testament are called the Gospels. They are Matthew, Mark, Luke and John. The word 'gospel' means 'good news.' These four books tell the good news about Jesus Christ, the Son of God. The good news is that God sent his Son into the world to be our Lord and Saviour. The Gospels focus on the life, death and resurrection of Jesus.

The Gospels were written to help people have faith in Jesus and to walk in faith with Jesus throughout their lives. One Gospel writer called John said that 'In the presence of his disciples, Jesus did many miracles which are not written down in this book. But these things have been written that you may believe that Jesus is the Christ, the Son of God, and that through faith in him, you might have eternal life.'

# FEEDING THE MULTITUDE
## From Matthew 14, Mark 6, Luke 9 & John 6

The feast of the Passover was approaching. A large crowd of about 5000 men, not including the number of women and children, followed Jesus and the disciples into the wilderness. Jesus saw the crowd and asked Philip, 'Where shall we buy bread for these people to eat?' Jesus was testing Philip, because he already knew what he was going to do.

Philip remarked, 'Two hundred **denarii** wouldn't even cover the cost.'

Andrew, the brother of Simon Peter, said to Jesus, 'There is a lad here who has five loaves and two small fish. But that's not enough to go around so many people.'

Jesus told his disciples, 'Get everyone to sit down.'

They all sat down on a large area of grass.

Taking the loaves and the two small fish, Jesus gave thanks and gave them to his disciples

to give out to the people. When they had all eaten as much as they wanted, Jesus commanded his disciples, 'Pick up the pieces that remain so that nothing is lost.'

The disciples did as Jesus told them, and they filled twelve baskets with the pieces of bread and fish that were not eaten.

When the crowd saw the miracle that Jesus performed they exclaimed, 'This must be the Prophet who was to come into the world!'

Jesus realised that the people were about to come and forcefully make him their king. So, he went off again to the mountain to be by himself.

## WHAT'S THE POINT:

Jesus miraculously provided bread and fish to the hungry, showing that he was able to provide what was needed to sustain or support life. The miracle was a sign pointing to Jesus as the only one who can provide what is needed for life in this world, and the next. Apart from Jesus, there is no true life at all.

## LOOK BACK:

Read Exodus 16:1-36

God gave his grumbling people bread from heaven, day after day, as they wandered in the wilderness. God is the generous provider of all we need for life.

## LOOK FORWARD:

Read John 6:35-39

Without bread you die. Without Jesus, the Bread of Life, you are dead spiritually and eternally.

## CHECK THIS OUT:

Read Deuteronomy 18:15-18, and Acts 3:22-23

Moses said that another prophet would rise from among the Jewish people. This prophet would speak the Word of God and so everyone must listen to him. Peter identified the prophet as Jesus Christ. We must listen to Jesus and do as he says.

## THINK:

Jesus knew the crowd had not grasped what sort of king he was. Jesus was not going to set them free from their Roman overlords and provide them with bread every day. This was what the people expected a king to do for them. What sort of king did Jesus come to be? Is Jesus the king you want?

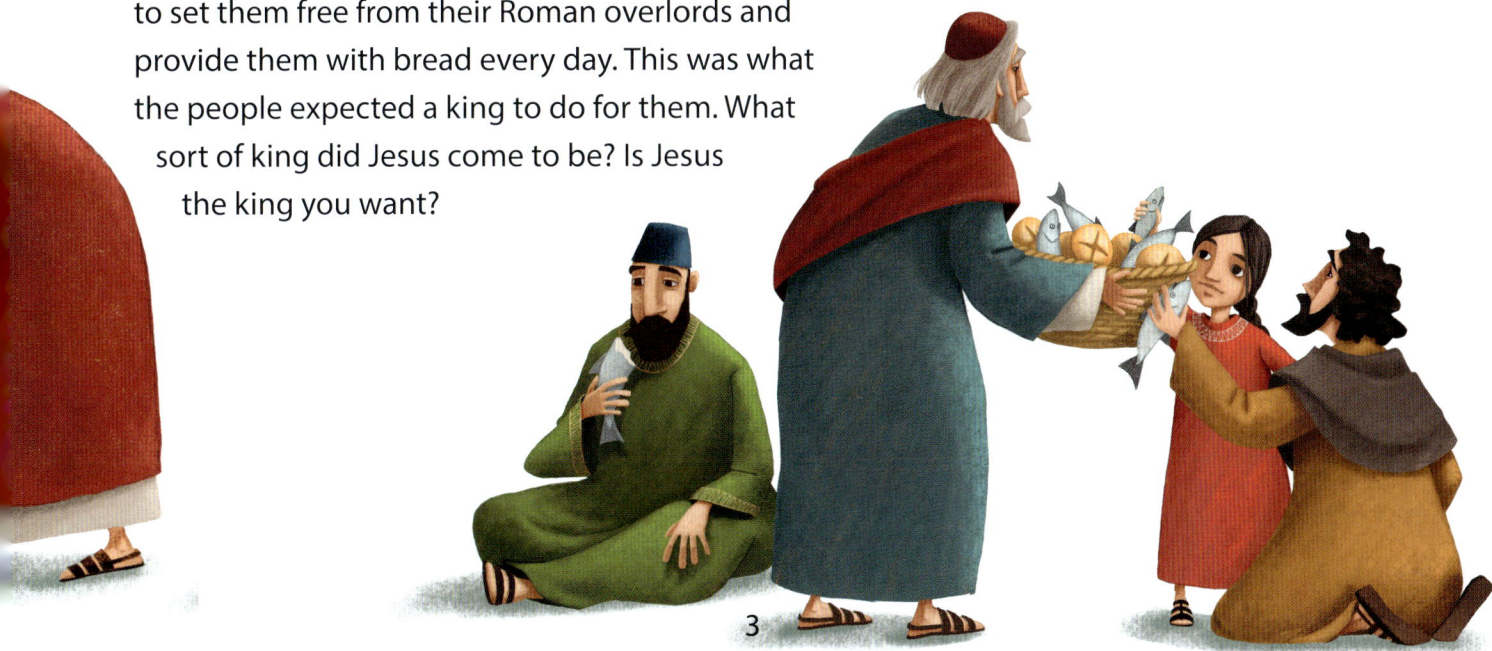

# A WALK ON WATER

## From Matthew 14, Mark 6 & John 6

Jesus told his disciples to get into the boat and go to the other side of the lake ahead of him, while he sent the large crowd away. Afterwards he went up the mountain to pray on his own to his heavenly Father.

When the boat was a long way off from land a storm came quickly and the boat was tossed about by the wind and waves. At dawn, Jesus came towards his disciples

in the boat. He was walking on the water. When the disciples saw him they were confused and petrified.

'It's a ghost!' they shrieked.

Jesus shouted to his disciples. 'It is I; fear not.'

Peter yelled, 'If that is you, Lord, let me to come to you on the water!'

'Come to me,' Jesus commanded him.

Peter got out of the boat. He started to walk on the water and approached Jesus. Then Peter became scared when he saw the strong wind, and he began to sink.

'Lord, save me!' he screeched.

Jesus reached out his hand and caught hold of Peter.

'What little faith you have, Peter. Why did you hesitate?'

Jesus and Peter got back into the boat. Immediately the wind stopped. Then the disciples in the boat worshipped Jesus, declaring aloud, 'You are truly the Son of God!'

## WHAT'S THE POINT:

Jesus walked on the water as if it were dry land. Everything is under his control. Jesus revealed himself to his disciples as 'I Am,' the name given to God in the Old Testament. Therefore, there is no need to be afraid, for God in Christ is with us. Did you notice that Peter didn't need to walk on the water. He just wanted to do something that Jesus was doing. Jesus shared his power and included Peter in what he was doing, even though Peter was weak and hesitated. Jesus did this to teach his followers that he is willing to include us in his mission to the world.

## LOOK BACK:

Read Genesis 1:1-2 and Psalm 78:13

In the Old Testament, the waters represented the powers of chaos. Only God himself has power and control over them. Only God can walk over the waters. What does that tell us about Jesus?

## THINK:

Do Jesus' words to his disciples encourage you to trust him through any challenges you face?

# WHO AM I?
## From Matthew 16, Mark 8 & Luke 9

Jesus and his disciples travelled to Caesarea Philippi. It was here that Jesus asked his disciples an extremely important question.

'Who do people say that I am?'

'Some people say that you are John the Baptist,' they answered. 'Others think you are Elijah the prophet,' they continued. 'There are some who say you are the prophet Jeremiah, or one of the other prophets of old,' they added.

Jesus asked his disciples directly. 'Who do you say I am?'

Peter declared, 'You are the Christ, the Son of the living God!'

'Do not tell anyone,' Jesus commanded his disciples. He explained to them that he must go to Jerusalem and suffer many terrible things at the hands of the Jewish religious leaders there. He will be killed, but he will rise from the dead on the third day.

Taking Jesus to one side, Peter began to scold Jesus for the things he was saying.

'This cannot be true,' Peter said. 'This will not happen to you.'

Jesus turned around and saw his disciples looking at them. 'Go away from me Satan!' he said sharply to Peter. 'You are not thinking about the things of God, but of men.'

Then Jesus spoke to the rest of his disciples. 'If anyone wants to be my disciple, he must reject his own selfish desires, take up his cross and follow me. Whoever wants to save his own life will surely lose it. But whoever loses his life for me and for the sake of the gospel will find it. How does it benefit anyone to gain everything the world has to offer but lose his soul in the process? What can anyone give in exchange for his soul? So, if you are ashamed of me and my words among these unfaithful and sinful people, then the Son of Man will

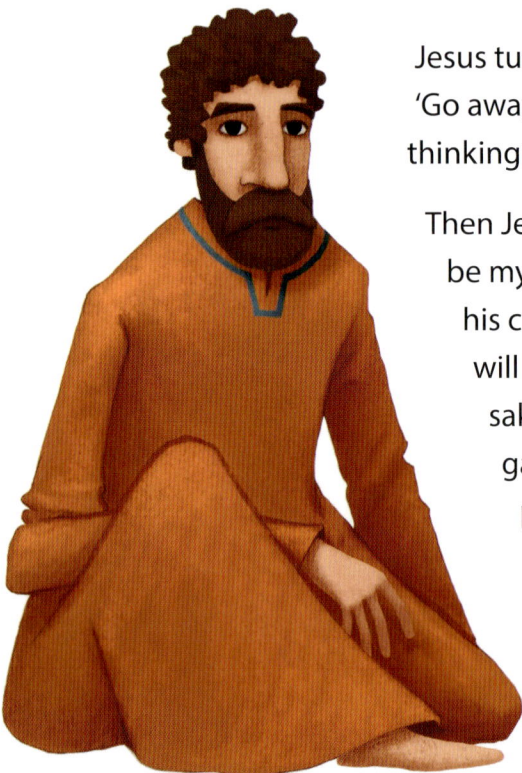

be ashamed of you, when he returns in his Father's glory with his holy angels.'

## WHAT'S THE POINT:

There were many opinions about who Jesus was, but only Peter declared the truth. Jesus is the Christ of God. Knowing the truth about who Jesus is and why he came is the most important thing to know. A wrong view of Jesus leads to a wrong view of discipleship.

## LOOK BACK:

Read 2 Samuel 7:5-16

The Old Testament spoke of a Messiah who would come as a great Saviour and King from the family line of David. He would lead and teach and save God's people.

## CHECK THIS OUT:

Read John 1:41 and John 4:25

The word 'Christ' is the Greek translation of the Hebrew word 'Messiah.' Both words simply mean 'Anointed One.' Peter confessed that Jesus is the One whom God has anointed as King over all creation.

## THINK:

Who do you say Jesus is?

# THE TRANSFIGURATION
## From Matthew 17, Mark 9 & Luke 9

Jesus took Peter, James, and his brother John up high on a mountain to pray. When Jesus began to pray, his face was suddenly **transfigured**, and his clothes became gleaming white.

Two men who looked like prophets of long ago suddenly appeared. One was Moses who led the Israelites out of slavery in Egypt and to the Promised Land. The other was Elijah, a truly great prophet of God. They spoke to Jesus about his departure – his impending death, resurrection, and ascension into heaven, which was soon going to take place in Jerusalem.

Peter and the other disciples were incredibly sleepy. But when they saw the amazing transformation of Jesus and the two men who were with him, they became instantly alert.

It looked as though Moses and Elijah were leaving Jesus, so Peter piped up, 'Master! It is good that we are here! Please allow us to make three tents – one for you, and one for Moses and one for Elijah.'

Peter was so overwhelmed by what he was seeing that he did not really know what he was talking about. As he was speaking, a cloud encompassed them, and a voice spoke to them from the cloud. 'This is my Son. He is my Chosen One. Keep listening to him.'

When the disciples heard the voice, they were gripped with fear and fell on their faces. As soon as the voice had finished speaking, Jesus told them to get up. They immediately saw that he was all alone.

Jesus asked his disciples not to tell anyone what they had seen or heard on the mountain, until after his resurrection from the dead.

## WHAT'S THE POINT:

Peter and the other disciples received a spectacular preview of Jesus's glory. Jesus is God in the flesh. We have the Father's word that Jesus is his Son. Jesus is the Chosen One we

are to listen to.
Jesus' disciples will
experience suffering
in this world of sin.
But as we trust and
obey Jesus, we have
his promise that
we, like Moses
and Elijah,
will share
in his glory in
heaven.

## LOOK BACK:

Read Exodus
33:18-23 and 34:6-7

Moses asked
God to show him God's glory. God's glory
is concerned with his goodness. God
proclaimed his name before Moses
which means that God's glory is
also something that can be heard!
Moses doesn't see all of God's glory,
because that would destroy him. But God
told Moses what it is that gives life - it is the
work of salvation.

## CHECK THIS OUT:

Read Exodus 12:29-42

Moses and Elijah spoke to Jesus about his
'departure.' The word means 'exodus.' It's the same word
that is used to describe how God saved his people from Egypt
in the Old Testament. God rescued his people from slavery and
brought them to freedom in the Promised Land. The 'exodus' that Jesus achieved
in Jerusalem came when he died on the cross to pay the price for our rebellion
against him – to rescue us and set us free from slavery to sin and the judgement we
deserve, and to bring us to heaven.

## LOOK FORWARD:

Read 2 Peter 1:16-18 and John 1:14

Don't listen to those who mock Jesus or his gospel. The Bible is God's Word. Christian truth
is based on the eyewitness testimonies of men, like John and Peter, who saw and heard
the Lord Jesus personally and wrote it down for us.

## THINK:

God told the disciples on the mountainside who Jesus is and how to live for Jesus every
day. What did God say to them? Will you do it too?

# WHO IS THE GREATEST?
## From Matthew 18, Mark 9 & Luke 9

Jesus and his disciples arrived at Peter's house in Capernaum. Once inside the house, Jesus asked them, 'What were you talking about among yourselves as you were walking along the road?'

The disciples did not answer Jesus. Instead, they said nothing out of shame because they had been arguing about which of them was the greatest disciple!

Jesus sat down and told the disciples, 'If anyone wants to be the greatest and have the place of honour, then he must be the slave of all and serve others.'

He took a little child and placed him in the middle of them. Jesus then lifted the child up in his arms and said, 'Anyone who welcomes such a little child as this in my name, welcomes me. What is more, whoever welcomes me, welcomes my Father who sent me. But if anyone causes one of my little followers to sin, it would be better for a large stone to be tied around the neck of that person and be thrown into the deepest sea!'

## WHAT'S THE POINT:

Greatness in the kingdom of God is about sacrifice and service. There is no room for pride. Followers of Jesus must serve him and his people wholeheartedly. The way to be great involves humbly serving and caring for others, including the weakest and poorest of God's people.

## CHECK THIS OUT:

Read Matthew 23:1-12

In Jewish life there was a preoccupation with status and position. The one who served others was seen as inferior. But Jesus taught his followers that in God's new community, the one who serves is the greatest. Jesus' followers must see others as more important and serve them in humility.

## THINK:

How do you become a great disciple of Jesus?

# THE GOOD NEIGHBOUR

## From Luke 10

One day, an expert in God's Law asked Jesus a hard question to test him. 'What must I do to get eternal life?' 'Well, you know God's Law. What does it say? How do you understand it?' Jesus asked him. 'Love the Lord your God with all your heart, and with all your soul, and with all your strength and with all your mind,' came the quick reply. 'And love your neighbour as you love yourself,' he added. Jesus responded, 'You have answered well. If you do this, you will have eternal life.'

But the lawyer wasn't satisfied, so he asked Jesus another question. 'Who is my neighbour?'

Jesus answered him with a parable. 'There was a man who travelled from Jerusalem to Jericho. He found himself surrounded by thieves who tore the clothes off him and gave him a severe beating. They left him for dead on the road and went on their way. Soon after, a priest was walking down that road. When he saw the poor man, he walked past him on the other side. The same thing happened when a **Levite** came walking by. Then a **Samaritan** arrived. When the Samaritan saw the poor man, he had mercy on him and helped him. He cleaned his wounds and bandaged them up. He then lifted him onto the back of his own beast and travelled to an inn where he continued to care for him. The following day he gave two denarii to the innkeeper and asked him to care for the injured man. "Look after him, and whatever more you spend on his care, I will pay you back when I return,"

'Then Jesus asked the lawyer, 'Which of these three men do you think was a neighbour to the poor man who was beaten by the thieves?' The lawyer replied, 'The one who had mercy on him.' Jesus told him, 'Well then, you go and do the same.'

## WHAT'S THE POINT:

The expert in God's Law wanted to know how to earn a place in heaven. Jesus taught him that he needed to live a perfect life to be good enough for God's kingdom. Of course, that was impossible because the man's heart was sinful and full of self-righteousness. We never love God and others, perfectly. We can never be good enough to get to heaven by our own good works. We need someone to rescue us from our slavery to sin and to offer us God's gift of eternal life. We need Jesus.

## LOOK BACK:

Read Leviticus 19:2, 18, 37 and Deuteronomy 6:5-7

There is only one true God, and he is holy. God's people must love him completely. They must treat God's Word seriously. Each person is to love his neighbour as himself.

## CHECK THIS OUT:

Read Deuteronomy 28:64-68, 1 Kings 11:1-13 and 2 Kings 17:24-31

When King Solomon turned from God and went after false gods, God was angry and split the nation into two kingdoms. These kingdoms were called Israel (10 tribes in the north) and Judah (2 tribes in the south). Israel and Judah had different kings. They often fought each other. God allowed the northern kingdom to be conquered by the Assyrians in 722 BC. The southern kingdom was conquered by the Babylonians in 586 BC. Both kingdoms were exiled from their land. In 722 BC, the Assyrian king brought foreigners to live in the Israelite city of Samaria. Some Jews had remained there, and they married the foreign Assyrians who were Gentiles. They also embraced Assyrian culture. So, the Samaritans had partly Jewish and partly Gentile ancestry. These differences meant there was a lot of bad feeling between them as well.

## THINK:

Do you love God and your neighbour? Can you be good enough to get to heaven without Jesus?

# COUNT THE COST
## From Matthew 10 & Luke 14

Large crowds were with Jesus, and he began to teach them about the cost of being his disciple.

'If you want to be my disciple, you must love me more than your father and mother and wife and children and brothers and sisters, and even your own life. If you do not love me more than these then you cannot be my disciple. Whoever does not deny himself and follow me wholeheartedly cannot be my disciple. If any of you wants to build a tower, do you not first of all sit down and work out if you can afford it so that you can finish the job? If you do not do this, you may not be able to complete the job once the foundation has been laid. Then everyone who sees what has happened will ridicule you. They will say, "This man started to build a tower but couldn't finish it!"

Or suppose a king is under the threat of war with another king. Will he not sit down first of all to work out if he can win the war with his army of ten thousand men against the other king's army of twenty thousand men? If he concludes that he cannot win, then he will send his ambassadors to the other king while he is a great distance away to negotiate terms of peace. So, if you want to be my disciple, you must give up everything you have and surrender your life to follow me.

Salt is good, but if it loses its saltiness, it is impossible to make it salty again. It is worthless, not fit for use in the soil or the dung heap, so it is thrown out. Those of you who can hear, listen carefully to what I am saying!'

## WHAT'S THE POINT:

What does it cost to be a Christian? Nothing, because God's mercy is freely offered. You could also say it costs a lot, because those who receive God's mercy surrender their lives to King Jesus. The two illustrations of the farmer and the king described the personal cost of following Jesus and encouraged the hearer to consider the cost. The man who built the tower was free to build or not. However, the king had a greater king coming against him. His choice was to be defeated or surrender. Therefore, consider the personal cost of following Jesus. And consider the dreadful cost of failing to surrender to the greatest king, Jesus Christ.

## CHECK THIS OUT:

Read Leviticus 2:13, Numbers 18:19, Job 6:6 and Luke 14:34-35

Salt was useful for many different things in the ancient world. The priests used it in sacrifices; to make covenants; to enhance flavour in food, and to mix into manure piles to make fertiliser. When speaking about discipleship though, Jesus challenged his hearers to be undeniably different in every way to the world. They have surrendered their lives completely to him and are useful in their service of Jesus, bringing glory to him.

## THINK:

To be a Christian, or not to be a Christian? That is the question!

# LOST PROPERTY

## From Luke 15

One day, a group of tax collectors and sinners gathered around Jesus to hear him preach the Word of God.

Some religious leaders, who were Pharisees and the scribes of the Law of Moses, complained that Jesus welcomed sinners into his company and loved to eat with them. Knowing that they were muttering about him, Jesus spoke to them in parables.

Jesus began, 'Which of you men, if he had a hundred sheep and lost one of them, would not leave the ninety-nine behind in the field, and search for the lost sheep until he found it? And when he found it, would not pick it up and lay it on his shoulders and return his lost sheep to his flock with great rejoicing in his heart? And when he got home, which of you men would not call his friends and neighbours

together for a party, telling them, "Rejoice with me, because I have found my lost sheep!" Well then, let me tell you that there is more rejoicing in heaven over one sinner who repents than over ninety-nine decent people who do not need to repent.

Or again, suppose a woman has ten silver coins and loses one of them. Will she not light a candle and sweep the whole house clean and look carefully for the lost coin until she finds it? And when she finds it, she gathers all her friends and neighbours together and tells them, "Rejoice with me because I have found my lost coin!" Well then, let me tell you again that there is more rejoicing by the angels of God in heaven when one sinner repents.'

## WHAT'S THE POINT:

The religious leaders did not like the company Jesus was keeping. So Jesus told them these parables to help them understand that their attitude to lost sinners was completely wrong. Jesus loves people so much that he searches for them to bring them into the kingdom of God. There is great rejoicing in heaven over every rebel who repents and turns back to him.

## LOOK BACK:

Read Ezekiel 34:1-31, Jeremiah 50:6 and Psalm 23:1-4 and 80:1.

The shepherds were the kings of Israel and Judah. They were appointed to rule on God's behalf, but they were corrupt, and their hearts were filled with pride. They only took care of their own needs and desires. God does not shepherd his flock that way. The Lord loves and takes care of his flock. God promised one shepherd from the ancestral line of David to rule over and care for his flock.

## CHECK THIS OUT:

Read John 10:11-18

Jesus identified himself as the promised Good Shepherd of the Old Testament. Jesus is the Good Shepherd who came to search for the lost, to bring back the strays, to bind up the injured, strengthen the weak and bring them home to heaven, at the cost of his own life on the cross.

## LOOK FORWARD:

Read 1 Peter 5:1-4

God's church needs good shepherds, or leaders, who are not like the wicked and powerful leaders of Israel and Judah. God's shepherds are to be godly, free of greedy and selfish motives, and able to take care of the church with loving gentleness and grace.

## THINK:

Are you happy when someone repents and turns back to God?

# LOST SON

## From Luke 15

Jesus told another parable to the people who had gathered about him.

He said, 'There was once a rich man who had two sons. The younger one said to his father, "Father, give me my portion of my inheritance." So, the man divided up all his goods and gave them to his sons. Shortly after, the younger son gathered together everything he had and journeyed to a far-away land where he wasted his money impetuously. Soon all his wealth was gone. Then a **famine** struck the land where the younger son was living, and he was completely destitute. He went to a local farmer to look for work and was sent out into the fields to care for the pigs. He was so hungry, he was ready to stuff himself with the husks that the pigs ate, because no one gave him anything to eat.

When he came to his senses, he said to himself, "How many of my father's hired workers have more than enough food to eat, and here I am dying of starvation! I am going to go back to my Father, and I will say to him, Father, I have sinned against heaven and before you. I am not worthy anymore to be called your son. Make me one of your hired workers instead."

The young man went back to his father. He was still a long way off when his father saw him. He was full of compassion for him. He ran to his son and hugged him with all

his might and kissed him. The
young son said to his father, "Father, I have
sinned against heaven and before you. I am not worthy anymore
to be called your son." Before he could say anything else, his father turned to his servants. "Quickly!" he said, "bring out the best robe you can find and put it on my son. Put a ring on his finger and shoes on his feet too. And bring out the prize calf and kill it. Let us feast and rejoice! For this son of mine was dead but now he lives; he was lost but now he is found." And so the celebrations began.

The father's eldest son was out working in the field. On his return to the house, he could hear music and dancing. "What's happening at the house?" he asked one of the hired workers.

"Your younger brother has returned," the worker told him, "and your father has killed the prize calf because he is safely home."

Arriving at the house, the older brother refused to go in because he was furious. His father came out and pleaded with him to join in the celebrations. But he said to his father, "Hold on, Father. I have served you diligently all these years and I have never disobeyed your instructions. And in all that time you have never given me so much as a young goat that I might have a party with my friends. But as soon as this other son of yours comes back, who has squandered his inheritance on **prostitutes**, you kill the prize calf for him!"

The father answered him, "My dear son, you are always here with me. Everything that is mine is also yours. However, it is right to be happy because your young brother was dead, but now he lives; he was lost, but now he is found.'"

## WHAT'S THE POINT:

The religious leaders rejoiced over lost property being found, but what about a lost soul being found by God? This parable shows how human beings, made in God's image, are separated from him because of their sin. The good news is that it

is possible to have a broken relationship with God restored, by turning back to him in real repentance. The younger brother was reconciled because he had the humility to repent. However, the pride of the older brother kept him away from the celebrations. His pride represented the pride of the religious leaders, who would eventually nail Jesus to a cross. Pride chooses hell over heaven. Pride gets in the way of a true relationship with God.

## LOOK BACK:

Read Psalm 119:176 and Isaiah 53:6

Sheep are known to wander towards danger. By nature, people are like sheep that will go astray and will never return home unless the Good Shepherd looks for them, gathers them together, and brings them home to the eternal fold.

## CHECK THIS OUT:

Read Deuteronomy 14:8

As they were God's chosen people, Israelites were to be different from the other nations. Their diets were also meant to be distinctive. Pigs were unclean animals. God's Law did not allow Jews to care for pigs or eat pork.

## THINK:

Is your relationship with God restored, or does pride in your heart keep it distant and broken?

# BE WISE WITH MONEY

## From Luke 16

Jesus told his disciples, 'Once there was a wealthy man who had a steward that looked after all his financial affairs. One day he was told that his steward was squandering his money, so he called him in and said, "What is this I hear about you wasting my money? Give me a complete account of how you have handled my money, for you are no longer fit to manage my finances."

The steward said to himself, "What am I going to do? My master is taking my job away from me. I'm not strong enough for manual labour, and I'm too ashamed to beg for a living."

He thought for a moment, then said, "I know what I'll do!" He hatched a plan so that he would still have friends who would welcome him into their homes when he no longer had his position with his wealthy master.

The steward called in all the people who were in debt to his master. "How much do you owe my master?" he asked the first one.

"About a hundred barrels of olive oil," the man replied.

"Here is your bill. Sit down quickly and write fifty barrels of olive oil instead."

The next person came in, and the steward asked, "And what about you – how much do you own my master?"

"Oh, about a hundred sacks of wheat," came the reply.

"Here is your bill. Take it quickly and write eighty sacks of wheat."

When the master heard what the steward had done, he was impressed and commended the steward for being shrewd. That's because the people of this world are much more shrewd in dealing with their own kind than are the people of the light.

So let me tell you how to use your worldly wealth. Use it to make friends for yourselves, so that when it's gone, you will be welcomed into the eternal home. The person who is trusted with little things will also be trusted with big things. In the same way, the person who is deceitful with little things is also deceitful with big things. If you have not been faithful in handling worldly wealth, who can trust you to handle true riches properly? And if you have not been honest in handling someone else's property, who can trust you with your own property?

No slave can serve two masters. Either he will hate one and love the other. Or he will be loyal to one and loathe the other. You cannot serve both God and money.'

## WHAT'S THE POINT:

It is easy to see if someone has real faith in Jesus by looking at what they do with their money. Christians should use money to glorify God. Therefore, invest your money in gospel ministry and mission.

## LOOK BACK:

Read Leviticus 27:30, Numbers 18:26-28 and 2 Chronicles 31:5

A **tithe** was a way of giving back to God what God first gave to his people.

## CHECK THIS OUT:

Read Luke 16:13, 2 Corinthians 9:6-7 and 1 Timothy 6:10

Money exercises a spiritual power over people. They exalt money and bow down to it as slaves. It kills them spiritually as they worship it. Jesus went to the cross to overpower everything that has enslaved us and to rescue anyone who puts their trust in him. We need to use our money for the same reason that Jesus came – to seek and to save the lost.

## THINK:

Will you give cheerfully and generously to the work of the gospel of Jesus in order to make an eternal difference in the lives of others?

# GETTING ETERNAL LIFE

## From Matthew 19, Mark 10 and Luke 18

Jesus and his disciples were travelling to Jerusalem. They entered a village in the region of Judea beyond the Jordan. Many people came to Jesus. He was famous because news of his miracles had spread throughout the area.

A rich young man ran up to him and fell on his knees before the Lord. 'Good Teacher, what do I have to do to receive eternal life?' he asked Jesus.

'Why do you call me good?' Jesus asked. 'Only God is good,' he reminded him. 'You know the commandments of God: "Do not commit adultery, do not murder anyone, do not steal, do not lie about other people, respect your father and mother."'

The young man assured Jesus, 'Yes, I have obeyed all these commandments from when I was a boy, so what am I missing?'

Jesus answered him. 'There is one thing that you still need to do. You need to sell all that you have and give the proceeds to the poor, and you will have riches in heaven. Then come and follow me.'

When the young man heard this, he went away deeply saddened because he was incredibly rich.

Jesus turned to his disciples and told them, 'It is extremely hard for the rich to enter the kingdom of God! It is easier for a camel to go through the eye of a needle than it is for a rich person to enter the kingdom of God!'

The disciples were stunned by what Jesus had revealed to them. 'Then who can be saved?' they asked.

Jesus replied, 'What is impossible for people to do, well, it is possible for God.'

Peter spoke up. 'Look, we have left everyone and everything to follow you, Lord. Don't forget that!'

Jesus said to them, 'Listen carefully because I am telling you the truth. Anyone who leaves home or family for the sake of the kingdom of God will receive much more in this life, and eternal life in the age to come.'

## WHAT'S THE POINT:

The rich young ruler had everything, but he was enslaved to money. He loved money more than God. His encounter with Jesus ended in sadness. It is hard for those who are rich to have the humility to know that they are lost. They have set their hearts on something other than Jesus. Money gives the sense of security and life, but it comes between us and God. It is impossible for anyone to do anything to gain eternal life. Salvation and eternal life are only possible with Jesus. That is why he went to the cross – to obtain salvation for all who will believe and receive it as a gift.

## LOOK BACK:

Read Ezra 3:11, Psalm 25:7-8 and 34:8 and Nahum 1:7

The Old Testament declared that only God was good. By calling Jesus "good" the rich young man was saying something important about Jesus – that Jesus is God in the flesh. But the way the young man responded to Jesus showed he was only being polite, and did not know the true identity of Jesus.

## CHECK THIS OUT:

Read Exodus 20:1-3

The young man was not loving God with all his heart, mind, soul and strength. He had an **idol** in his life. The idol was his wealth. He was breaking the first commandment of God. Contrary to what he thought, the young man did not keep all of God's commandments.

## THINK:

Do you have an idol in your life? Is there anything that you must give up to truly follow Jesus?

# TRUE TREASURE
## From Luke 19

Jesus and his disciples arrived at Jericho. They were passing through on their way to Jerusalem. A man called Zacchaeus lived there. He was the chief tax collector in that town, and he was extremely wealthy. Zacchaeus wanted to see Jesus, to find out more about him. However, he was a small man and could not see Jesus because the crowd were blocking his view. The people of Jericho did not like Zacchaeus because he took lots of money from them in taxes. He gave some of the money to the Romans but kept the rest for himself. Zacchaeus decided to run ahead of the crowd. He climbed a large sycamore tree to see Jesus because he knew that Jesus would soon pass that way.

When Jesus looked up into the tree he saw Zacchaeus in the branches. Jesus called to him, 'Zacchaeus, come down from there quickly! I must stay at your house today.' Zacchaeus did what Jesus commanded. He quickly climbed down from the tree and joyfully welcomed Jesus.

The crowd that had gathered were annoyed when they saw what had happened. 'Jesus has gone to be the guest at the home of this despicable sinner,' they grumbled.

Zacchaeus stood up and declared to the Lord Jesus, 'Know this, Lord, that I will give half of my possessions to the poor. And if I have cheated anyone, I will repay them four times as much as I have taken.'

Jesus said to Zacchaeus, 'Salvation has come to this house today, because even Zacchaeus is a true child of Abraham. For the Son of Man came to seek and to save the lost.'

## WHAT'S THE POINT:

This is transformation in action. Zacchaeus started to care for the people whom he cheated. This was the proof that Jesus was more precious to him than anything else, even all his treasures. Jesus' mission is to seek and save the lost. You are lost if you have set your heart on something other than Jesus. Jesus is more precious than life itself. He is our salvation and our life. Jesus is our true treasure. Salvation is being found by Jesus. When Jesus finds someone, he never leaves them.

## CHECK THIS OUT:

Read Deuteronomy 21:22-23 and Galatians 3:13

Zacchaeus went up a tree to see Jesus. Jesus, however, came down from heaven, and then went up a tree (the cross) for Zacchaeus, and for everyone who will put their trust in him.

In Deuteronomy a curse of God was upon those who were disobedient. The 'cursed' were hanged on a tree. Christ became a curse for us by dying on a tree (or the cross).

## THINK:

Is Jesus your true treasure?

# LAZARUS, COME OUT!

## From John 11

Jesus and his disciples approached Bethany, a village not far from Jerusalem. Three of his closest friends lived there; Mary, her sister Martha and their brother Lazarus. Lazarus was seriously ill. His sisters knew that Jesus could make him better. They heard that Jesus and his disciples were on their way to Jerusalem. So, they sent Jesus a message, asking him to come and help.

When Jesus and his disciples reached Bethany, Lazarus had been dead for four days and was already buried in a tomb. Martha went out to meet Jesus, but Mary stayed at home.

'Jesus, if you had been here, my brother would not have died,' cried Martha when she met the Lord. 'But I know,' she continued, 'that even now, whatever you ask God for, he will give you.'

'Listen to me, Martha,' replied Jesus. 'Even though your brother has died, he will live again.'

'I know he will rise to life in the resurrection on the last day,' said Martha.

Jesus said to her, 'I am the resurrection and the life. Whoever believes in me shall live, even though he dies. And whoever lives and believes in me shall never die. Do you believe this?'

'Yes, I believe you, Lord,' replied Martha, 'because I believe you are the Messiah, the Son of God, who has come into the world.'

Martha went back home and told Mary that Jesus wanted to see her.

Mary was grief-stricken and fell down at Jesus' feet. 'Lord, if you had been here, Lazarus would not have died,' she wailed. The other mourners were crying loudly too. Jesus was upset that death had taken his friend.

'Where have you buried him?' asked Jesus softly.

'Come and see, Lord,' they answered.

Jesus wept.

They led Jesus and his disciples to the tomb. A stone covered its entrance.

Jesus commanded them, 'Lift the stone away.'

Martha said, 'Lord, there will be a bad smell, because he has been dead four days.'

Jesus replied, 'Did I not tell you that if you believed, you would see the glory of God?'

So they removed the stone. Then Jesus prayed aloud to God.

'Thank you, my Father, for always listening to my prayers. Let everyone now see that you have sent me to give life.'

After Jesus had prayed, he shouted, 'Lazarus! Come out!'

Lazarus appeared, wrapped in his grave clothes. He shuffled slowly out of the tomb and into the daylight.

'Take the grave clothes off him,' Jesus said to them. They rushed forward to help Lazarus. They were overjoyed because Lazarus, who was dead, was alive again!

## WHAT'S THE POINT:

The sisters were united in grief and in the belief that the Lord Jesus could have prevented their brother's death. Jesus was full of sympathy for them, and he mourned with them. When Jesus raised Lazarus from the grave, he was pointing to the final victory over death that he would win, through his own death on the cross and his resurrection in Jerusalem.

## LOOK BACK:

Read Ecclesiastes 3:4

There is a right time to mourn. Jesus wept before he encouraged Martha to look to him in faith. Jesus wept before he raised Lazarus. In the face of death, Jesus wept first. So should we – 'mourn with those who mourn'- Romans 12:15.

## CHECK THIS OUT:

Read Romans 8:38-39 and 1 Corinthians 15:55-57

In raising Lazarus, Jesus gave a preview of the full and final victory over death, hell, and Satan – that is what his cross achieves for all who trust in him. Not only has death lost its sting, it can never separate us from God!

## THINK:

Jesus said, 'I am the resurrection and the life. Whoever believes in me, though he dies, yet shall he live, and everyone who lives and believes in me shall never die.' Do you believe this? Where is your trust as you face your own mortality?

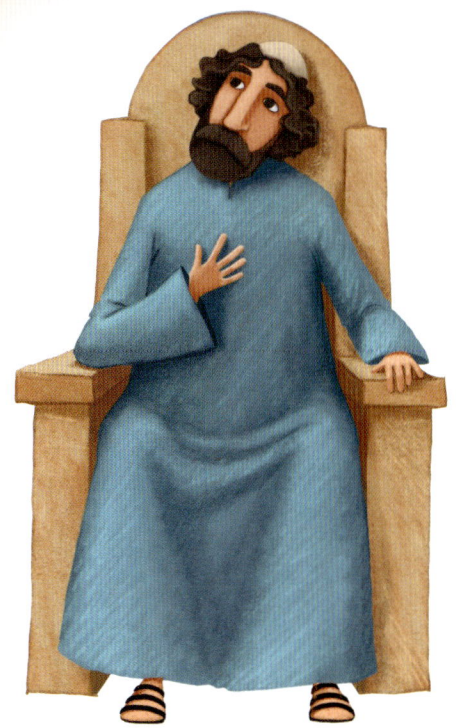

# A BAD REQUEST

## From Mark 10

Jesus and his followers were on the road to Jerusalem. Jesus was walking way out in front of his disciples. They were alarmed because of what Jesus had told them was going to happen to him there. The others who followed were also afraid.

Jesus took his disciples aside and began to tell them again what was going to happen to him in Jerusalem. He explained that he would be arrested by the Jewish religious leaders. They will sentence him to death and give him to the Gentiles who will deal with him harshly. The Gentiles will ridicule him and assault him and kill him.

'Then after three days, I will rise to life again,' Jesus told them. After he had said these things, he walked ahead of them once more.

James and John caught up with him because they wanted to ask him a question in private.

'Teacher, we want you to do something for us.'

'What do you want me to do for you?'

'When you come into your kingdom, and sit on your throne, we want you to seat us at either side of you – one on your right, and the other on your left.'

'You have no idea what you are asking. Can you drink the cup that I drink? Can you be baptised with the same baptism as me?'

'We can!'

'You will drink the cup that I drink, and you will be baptised with the same baptism as me. But I cannot do what you ask. These places have already been prepared by my Father.'

The other disciples overheard the conversation and became extremely cross with James and John. So, Jesus called them all together and said to them, 'The men who are considered rulers of the Gentiles have power over the people and their leaders have authority over them. But this is not to be the way among you. If one of you wants to be great, then he must be a servant. And if one of you wants to be first, then he must be the servant of everyone else. You must understand that even the Son of Man did not come into this world to be served but to serve and to give his life to rescue many people.'

## WHAT'S THE POINT:

People want power. They want to be greater than others. People who are great in the world's eyes have status. They get to the top by trampling on others. They want glory and adoration. But Jesus tells his disciples that they are not to be like that. Jesus is the servant king. Jesus came to redeem us and create a new humanity with a different value system to the world. Jesus expects his followers to be actively serving others.

## LOOK BACK:

Read Genesis 6:11-18, Exodus 14:26-29, Isaiah 51:17, 22 and Jeremiah 25:15

The cup of God's wrath was against those who rebelled against him. The baptism image was one of judgement, that is, being completely overwhelmed by the waters of God's judgement which he declared on humanity because they rebelled against him. Jesus told his disciples that they will indeed experience suffering. They will not die for anyone's sins, like Jesus, but they will suffer for loving and following him and for God's glory.

## THINK:

As a Christian, are you serving people at home, in school, at church, and in the community?

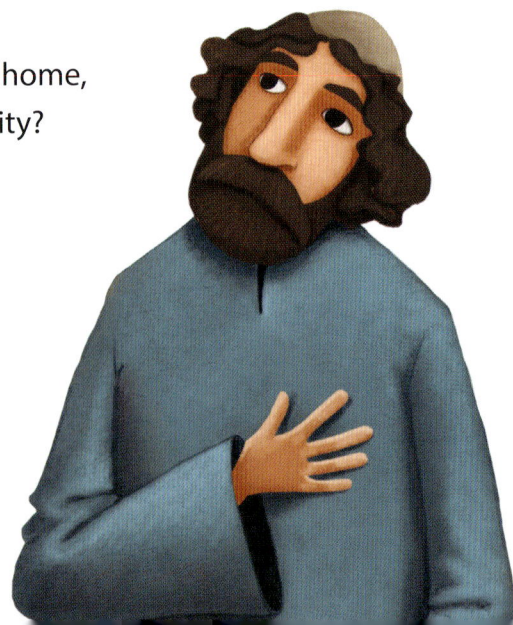

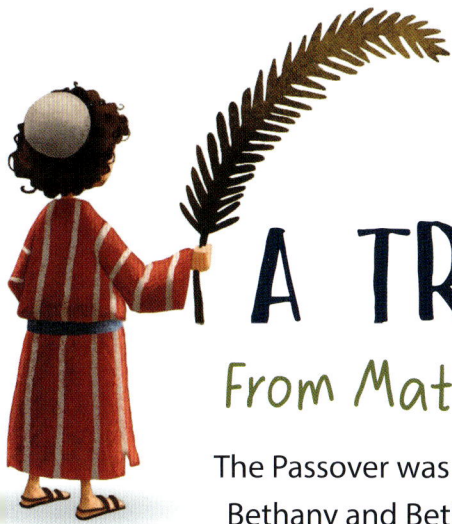

# A TRIUMPHANT ENTRY

## From Matthew 21, Mark 11, Luke 19, & John 12

The Passover was approaching. Jesus and his disciples came to the villages of Bethany and Bethpage, near Jerusalem. At a place called the Mount of Olives, Jesus sent two of his disciples to a nearby village and gave them instructions on what to do when they got there.

'When you enter the village you will see a young donkey that is tied up, that no one has ever ridden before,' Jesus told them. 'Untie it and bring it to me. If anyone asks you, "Why are you untying the young donkey?" tell them, "The Lord needs it and will return it when he is done with it."'

This was to fulfil the words of the prophet from long ago, who declared, 'Proclaim in the city of Jerusalem, "Look! Your King is coming to you! He is humble, and he rides in on a colt, a young donkey."'

The two disciples went on their way and found the colt tied up at a door out in the street. Some people in the street watched the disciples untie it.

As soon as the disciples started to loosen the ropes, they were challenged. 'What are you doing? Why are you are untying that young donkey?' the people asked them.

The disciples replied, 'The Lord needs it.'

The people looked at each other. They looked at the young donkey. They looked at the disciples. 'Well, that's okay then,' they said, and they let the disciples return to Jesus with the young donkey trotting behind them.

They brought the colt to Jesus. The disciples laid their garments on its back to make a saddle for Jesus to sit on. As Jesus set off for Jerusalem, many people spread their cloaks on the road while others laid down leafy branches that they had cut from fields.

Everyone started to praise him by shouting, 'Hosanna to the Son of David! Blessed is the King that comes in the name of the Lord! Hosanna in the highest!'

When Jesus entered Jerusalem, the whole city was excited by his coming. 'Who is this?' they wondered.

The crowds declared, 'This is the prophet Jesus
from the town of Nazareth in Galilee!'

Jesus went into the temple. He looked around at everything, but as it was late in the day, and the place was so crowded, he returned to Bethany with his twelve disciples to stay with friends for the night.

## WHAT'S THE POINT:

Jesus was in complete control of the events leading to his death in Jerusalem. As he entered the city, Jesus was hailed as God's new king who had come to rescue his people. They shouted 'Hosanna,' which means 'Lord save us!' The people wanted a king who would free them from the control of Rome, but Jesus came to fulfil the Scriptures. Jesus came to set them free, not from Roman rule, but from the power and destructive consequences of sin. To be set free from sin people need only repent, trust in King Jesus, and know his gentle and loving rule in their lives.

## LOOK BACK:

Read Zechariah 9:9-10

The prophet told them that when God's promised king came to Jerusalem, he would enter the city on a young donkey. Jesus did not enter Jerusalem in pomp and ceremony. He came in gentleness. His kingly rule will be over all the earth.

## CHECK THIS OUT:

Read Psalm 118:25-29

This Psalm was traditionally sung during the period of the Passover. It was a prayer of blessing for the coming kingdom of the Messiah. The crowd rightly applied the words of the Psalm to Jesus the Messiah as he entered Jerusalem.

## THINK:

Do you praise and thank Jesus that he is God's king, who came into the world to die for you and save you?

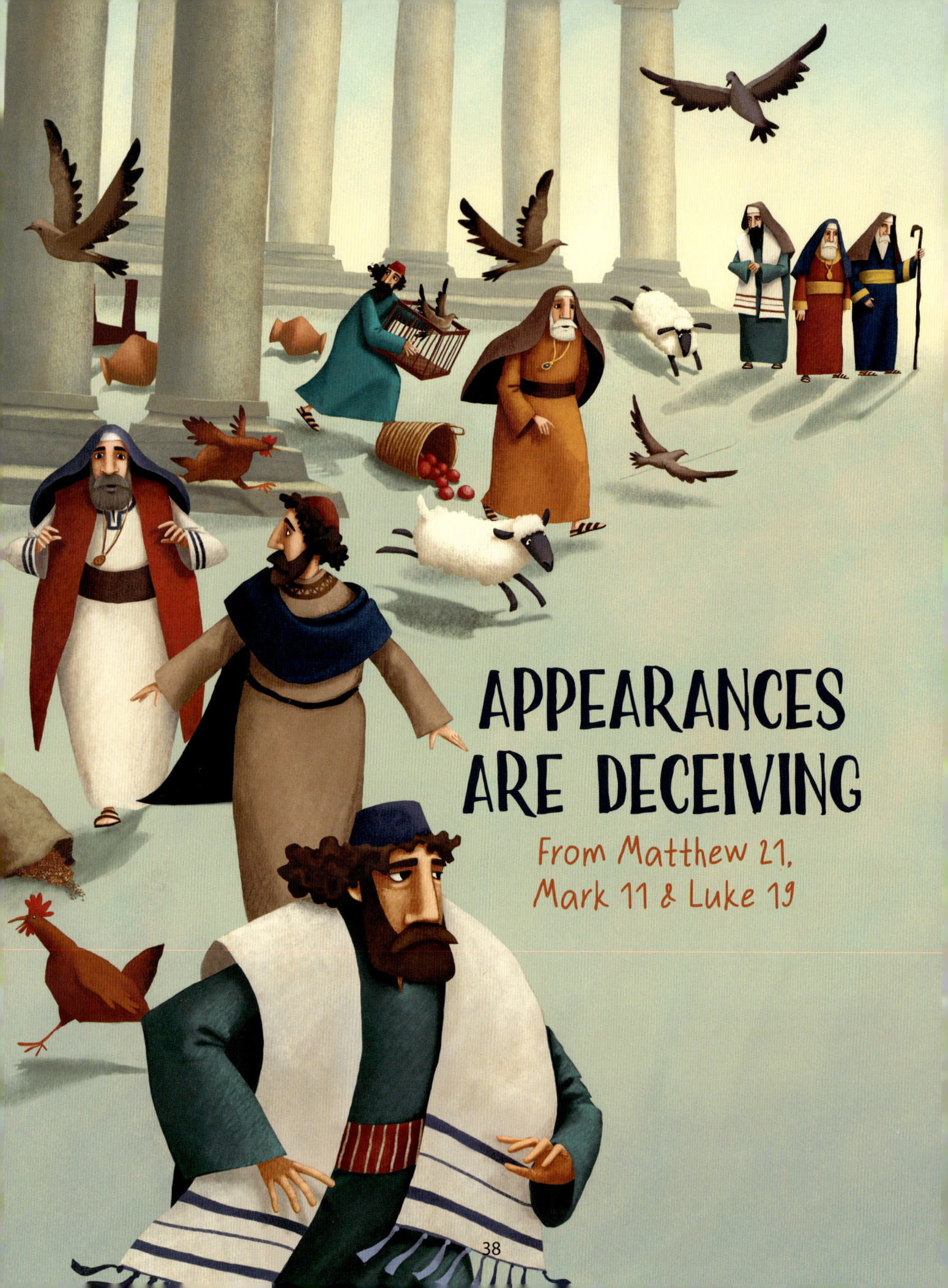

# APPEARANCES ARE DECEIVING

From Matthew 21,
Mark 11 & Luke 19

The next day, Jesus and his disciples left Bethany and headed for Jerusalem. He was hungry and seeing a fig tree with leaves on it, he went to find out if any fruit was growing on it. But there was nothing, as it wasn't the right time of year for figs. Jesus cursed the tree, saying, 'May no one ever eat any fruit from you again.' The disciples heard what Jesus said to the fig tree but said nothing.

Soon after, they arrived in Jerusalem. Jesus went straight into the temple. He started to drive out anyone who bought and sold things in the temple. He overturned the tables of the money changers and the seats of the dove sellers. He stopped people carrying anything through the courtyards of the temple.

Jesus then taught the people the Scriptures. He proclaimed to them, 'My house shall be called a house of prayer for all the nations. But you have made it a hiding place for thieves!'

The chief priests and the teachers of the Law of Moses were furious. They started looking for a way to kill Jesus. They were afraid of Jesus because the crowds of people were amazed at what he was teaching them.

That evening, Jesus and his disciples left the city and went back to Bethany.

The next morning, Jesus and his disciples were walking along the road into Jerusalem, and they saw the fig tree that Jesus cursed the day before. It was completely dead!

Peter exclaimed, 'Teacher, look! The fig tree you cursed is dead!'

'You must have faith in God,' Jesus told his disciples. 'I am telling you the truth, whoever tells this mountain to throw itself into the sea, and does not doubt it in his heart, then it will happen. In the same way, when you pray and ask God for something, believe that you have received it, and you will get whatever you have asked for. And when you stand up to pray, forgive whatever you have against someone else, so that your Father in heaven may forgive you for your sins.'

## WHAT'S THE POINT:

The fig tree looked like it was full of fruit, but on closer inspection by Jesus, it was fruitless. It was a picture of the temple in Jerusalem. The temple was noisy and busy. It seemed to be full of life. It looked good on the outside, but it was rotten to the core. The temple had become a hideaway for thieves and con artists. It was full of false worshippers. It was flashy but fruitless. The religious leaders were full of pride and looked for a way to kill Jesus, the giver of true life. They did not have faith in Jesus. Without faith, it is impossible to please God, so put your faith in him. Be a true worshipper of Jesus.

## LOOK BACK:

Read Isaiah 56:7 and Jeremiah 7:11

God's people were sinful and worshipped false gods. Having confessed their sins in the temple, they would leave to continue in their wicked ways. Jesus spoke the words of the prophets to emphasise the people's sin and his righteous anger at them for being false worshippers of the only true God.

## LOOK FORWARD:

Read Hebrews 7:22-28, 9:26 and 12:22-24

There is one true sacrifice for sin, and one true temple that brings about good fruit for all eternity. Jesus' death on the cross is the full and sufficient sacrifice for sin. Jesus is the true temple where God is worshipped and glorified. If you want to worship God, come to Jesus.

## CHECK THIS OUT:

Read Jeremiah 8:13, 24:1-10 and Hosea 9:10

Sometimes the people of Israel were represented as figs on a fig tree, or as a fig tree that produced no fruit. God looks for fruit, that is, for good works in keeping with our love and faith in him.

## THINK:

Appearances can be deceiving. Are you a true worshipper of Jesus, or do you just look like one?

# ARE YOU READY?

## From Matthew 25

Jesus sat on the Mount of Olives. His disciples were with him, and he began to teach them what the kingdom of God is like. He said, 'One evening, ten bridesmaids took their lamps and went to meet the bridegroom. Five of the women were foolish and the other five were wise. The foolish ones took their lamps, but they did not bring any extra oil with them. The wise ones, however, took extra containers full of oil with them.

The bridegroom was late. The women grew tired and fell asleep. Suddenly, at midnight, there was a loud announcement. "The bridegroom has arrived! Go out and meet him!"

The bridesmaids woke up and got their lamps ready. The foolish bridesmaids said to the wise, "Give us some of your oil because our lamps are starting to go out."

"We cannot give you some of our oil," replied the wise bridesmaids. "If we did, there would not be enough for all of us. You should go and buy some oil from the traders for yourselves."

So, the foolish bridesmaids went off to buy oil. While they were away, the bridegroom finally arrived. The bridesmaids who were ready went into the marriage feast with him. Then the doors were shut. Soon after, the other bridesmaids arrived.

"Lord, Lord, open the doors for us!" the foolish bridesmaids cried out. But the bridegroom replied, "I am truthfully telling you; I do not know who you are!"

Therefore, be ready, because you do not know the day or hour that the Son of Man will return.'

## WHAT'S THE POINT:

Jesus used a wedding to explain his second coming and how important it is that we should be ready when he returns. No one knows when Jesus will return. People have no control over the timing of it. It is impossible to be a citizen of the kingdom of God and live a lifestyle of foolishness, laziness, and wickedness. And the point of the oil in the parable? No one can rely on the readiness of someone else. If you are not a Christian, you won't get into heaven because you have a relative who is. When Jesus returns, you must know him personally. The day of his return will end history, and everyone will stand before Jesus as Judge. Therefore wake up and be ready – the bridegroom is coming soon!

## LOOK BACK:

Read Isaiah 54:4-6 and Isaiah 62:5

God referred to himself as the bridegroom of his bride, Israel. God desires to be with his people. God wants to share time and be close to his people, like a groom does his bride.

## CHECK THIS OUT:

Read Matthew 9:14-15

Jesus chose the image of the bridegroom for himself because he is 'God with us' and he loves his bride, the Church.

## THINK:

One day (we don't know when) Jesus will come again and close the doors of heaven so that those inside will enjoy untroubled fellowship with him forever. Which side of the door will you be on?

# JUDAS THE BETRAYER
## From Matthew 26, Mark 14 & Luke 22

When Jesus finished teaching his disciples, he said to them, 'It is the feast of the Passover in two days. At that time, the Son of Man will be betrayed and crucified.'

Meanwhile, the chief priests and the Jewish elders met in the palace of Ciaphas the High Priest. They came up with a strategy to arrest Jesus quietly and murder him. 'We must not do it during the Passover,' they said to each other. 'We don't want the people to riot!'

Satan had entered Judas Iscariot, one of the twelve disciples. Judas went to the chief priests and asked, 'What will you give me if I betray Jesus and hand him over to you?'

The chief priests talked amongst themselves and agreed on a price. They counted out thirty pieces of silver and gave the money to Judas. From that moment on, Judas looked for the right moment to betray Jesus and hand him over to the Jewish religious leaders.

## WHAT'S THE POINT:

The chief priests decided that Jesus must die. They had not read nor understood the Scriptures properly. These religious men should have known and believed in Jesus Christ. One of Jesus' disciples, Judas, should also have believed, considering everything he heard and witnessed while he was with Jesus. These men lacked the proper response to Jesus. A life of faith in Jesus is the proper response to God's Chosen One.

## CHECK THIS OUT:

Read John 5:39-47

The religious leaders did not read the Scriptures with their minds open to be led by the Spirit of God. They had a wrong view about Jesus. Their corrupt religious system meant that they had grown away from God. They didn't see their need for him. Jesus was a threat, so they must kill him – the One about whom Scripture is written!

## THINK:

Have you ever betrayed Jesus? How did you feel?

# THE LAST SUPPER
## From Matthew 26, Mark 14 & Luke 22

It was time for the Passover. Jesus sent two disciples into the city to prepare for the Passover feast. Jesus told them, 'When you get to the city, you will find a man carrying a jar of water. Follow him to a house and say to the owner, "The Master wants to know where your guest room is so that he can eat the Passover feast with his disciples." He will show you to a large furnished room upstairs. Prepare the Passover feast there.'

The men left and found things exactly as Jesus had told them. They prepared the Passover feast in the upstairs room.

In the evening, Jesus sat down at the table with his disciples. As they were eating, Jesus took some bread, gave thanks, and blessed it. He broke it and gave it to his disciples. 'Take and eat it,' he said, 'for this is my body which is given for you. Remember me when you do this.'

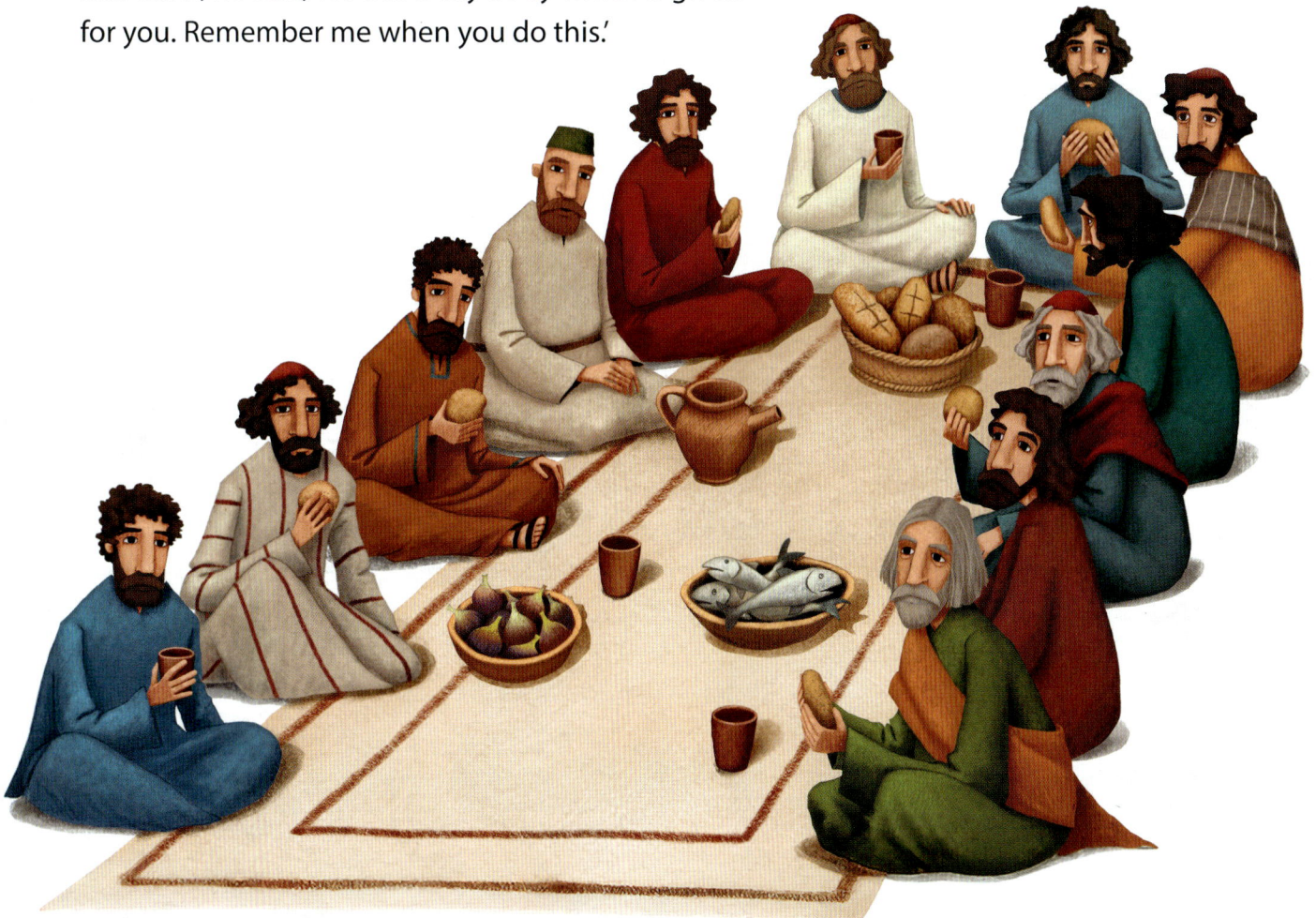

Jesus took a cup of wine and gave thanks to God. Then he passed it to his disciples. 'Drink this, all of you,' he said. 'This is my blood of the new covenant, which is shed for you and for many for the forgiveness of sins. I will not drink the fruit of the vine again until I drink it new with you in the kingdom of my Father.'

They sang a hymn. When they were finished, Jesus and his disciples went out to the Mount of Olives.

## WHAT'S THE POINT:

The last meal Jesus ate with his disciples was **symbolic** of the events that were going to take place the next day. The bread broken represented his crucified body. The wine poured out represented his blood shed on the cross. We can enter into a new and restored relationship with God through the death of Jesus, his only Son.

## LOOK BACK:

Read Exodus 13:4-10

God gave the Israelites a special meal to eat every year called the Passover. It helped them remember the awesome power of God as he rescued his people out of slavery in Egypt. This rescue pointed to a greater rescue as Jesus, the Lamb of God, shed his blood on a cruel cross to rescue his people forever from slavery to sin, the world and the devil.

## CHECK THIS OUT:

Read 1 Corinthians 10:16-17 and 11:23-29

The Lord's Supper is meant to demonstrate the unity of a church. It is a means of deep fellowship with Jesus and his people. We must never treat the Lord's Supper disrespectfully or take it while there is unconfessed sin in our hearts.

## THINK:

Jesus died to **ransom** people from every tribe and language and nation. One day, they will all be in heaven. Jesus will then feast joyfully with his redeemed people. Will you be at the feast?

# GETHSEMANE
## From Matthew 26, Mark 14, Luke 22 & John 18

'Tonight you will all desert me,' Jesus told his disciples as they walked to the Mount of Olives.

'Even if the rest leave you, Lord, I will never do that!' asserted Peter.

'I'm telling you the truth, Peter, that before the cock crows, you'll have denied knowing me three times.'

Peter exclaimed, 'Not at all Lord! Even if I have to die with you, I will not deny you!'

The others agreed, as they felt the same way as Peter.

Jesus and his disciples reached the Garden of Gethsemane, at the foot of the Mount of Olives. 'Wait here. I'm going over there to pray,' he said.

Peter, James, and John went with Jesus a short distance. Jesus' heart was full of sorrow. Jesus told the three men, 'Remain here and watch with me.' Walking a little farther, Jesus fell on his knees and prayed earnestly to his heavenly Father that he would not have to suffer. 'If it is possible, Father, take this cup of wrath from me. Yet, let not my will but your will be done.'

Jesus returned to where Peter, James, and John were waiting. They were fast asleep. Jesus asked, 'Could you not have stayed awake with me just one more hour?' Jesus went to pray again and returned only to find the three disciples sleeping again. This time he did not wake them. He prayed some more, saying the same thing to his Father each time.

When he returned to where the three disciples slumbered, Jesus said, 'Are you still sleeping? Wake up! Look! The time has come for the Son of Man to be handed over into the hands of sinful men. My betrayer is here.'

Judas Iscariot led a crowd with clubs and swords. He told them, 'The man I kiss is the one you want to arrest.' When Judas kissed Jesus on the cheek, the crowd rushed forward and seized Jesus. Peter cut of the ear of the high priest's servant with his sword.

'Put your sword away!' Jesus commanded. He touched the man's ear and healed him.

'All who live by the sword will die by the sword,' continued Jesus. 'If I wanted to remain free, I could appeal to my Father, and armies of angels would fight for me. But how would the Scriptures be fulfilled if I did that?

Jesus then spoke to the crowds. 'Why have you come here brandishing swords and clubs, as if I am a violent criminal? Every day I sat in the temple teaching you the Scriptures, and you did not arrest me. But this has happened to fulfil the Scriptures about me.'

Afraid, the disciples deserted Jesus and ran away.

## WHAT'S THE POINT:

In the Garden of Gethsemane, Jesus wrestled with the pain and agony of his **crucifixion**. Nevertheless, Jesus wanted his Father's will to be done, and not his own. Jesus was obedient to the will and plan of his Father to go to the cross to rescue sinners like us.

## LOOK BACK:

Read Isaiah 53:10 and Zechariah 13:7

The sword of the Lord's judgement went out against the good shepherd, scattering his flock. It wasn't because he deserved it but because he took responsibility for the sins of others.

## CHECK THIS OUT:

Read Jeremiah 25:15-29 and 2 Corinthians 5:21

The 'cup' was a symbol of God's wrath – his righteous anger against sin and his judgement on unrepentant sinners. Jesus drank the cup of God's wrath, not because he sinned (he never sinned) but because of humanity's sin.

## THINK:

Jesus was in control of the events in the Garden of Gethsemane. Do you believe that Jesus is in control of his world?

# I DON'T KNOW HIM!

## From Matthew 26, Mark 14, Luke 22 & John 18

Jesus was taken to the palace of the high priest. The Jewish religious leaders had gathered there. They decided that Jesus must stand trial. Meanwhile, Peter had followed the crowd into the courtyard of the high priest's palace. He could see Jesus through a window in the courtyard.

Peter went to warm himself by the fire in the middle of the courtyard. A servant girl noticed him.

'Weren't you also with Jesus the Galilean?' she asked him.

Peter replied, 'No. I don't know what you are talking about.' He moved away from the fire and walked to the entrance gate of the courtyard. Another servant girl saw him.

49

'That man over there, he was with Jesus of Nazareth,' she said to a group of bystanders as she pointed at Peter.

Peter overheard her comment. 'I promise you, I do not know the man,' he responded, and turned his back on them.

A while later, some of the bystanders approached Peter and looked closely at him. 'Without doubt, you are one of that man's friends. And you have the same accent that he does,' one of them said.

'Listen to me! I do not know that man!' Peter insisted.

At that moment, a cock crowed. Jesus turned and looked at Peter through the window. Peter remembered what Jesus had said to him only a few hours earlier, 'Before the cock crows, you'll have denied knowing me three times.'

Peter was totally ashamed of himself. He ran quickly out of the courtyard. He was deeply distressed and began to cry inconsolably.

## WHAT'S THE POINT:

Peter said he would stick with Jesus, even if it meant prison and death. But when trouble came, Peter denied knowing Jesus at all. It happened exactly as Jesus said it would. No wonder Peter wept uncontrollably. At times, we fail Jesus. We can be afraid to be counted as his. Thankfully, Jesus knows our weaknesses and is gracious towards us. Just look to the cross to see how much he loves us despite our failings.

## LOOK FORWARD:

Read Acts 4:1-4

Jesus forgave and restored Peter as an apostle and sent him out to proclaim the gospel boldly. Peter and John were arrested and put in prison for telling people the good news about Jesus. Peter was no longer afraid to suffer as a follower of Jesus.

## CHECK THIS OUT:

Read Psalm 145

When you stumble and fall in your Christian life, use this Psalm of David as a prayer. Thank God for being slow to anger, abounding in mercy and always willing to forgive you when you fail him.

## THINK:

Have you ever been too embarrassed to tell your friends that you are a Christian?

# ON TRIAL

## From Matthew 26-27, Mark 14-15, Luke 22-23 & John 18

Jesus was brought to the palace of Caiaphas, the high priest. The Jewish religious leaders had gathered there to put Jesus on trial. They called in several witnesses to falsely accuse Jesus because they wanted an excuse to kill him. None of them told the same story.

Caiaphas asked Jesus, 'Tell us, are you the Messiah, the Son of God?'

'I am,' Jesus answered, 'and all of you will see the Son of Man seated on the right hand of God Almighty, and coming with the clouds of heaven!'

Caiaphas was furious and tore his clothes. 'What further proof do we need? It is **blasphemy**!' He turned to the Jewish leaders and asked, 'What is your decision?'

'He deserves to die!' they responded angrily. Some of them spat at Jesus, while others hit him hard.

The Jewish leaders brought Jesus to Pontius Pilate, the Roman governor. Bound and badly beaten, Jesus stood before Pilate.

'This man is a menace to our people. He tells them not to pay taxes to Caesar, and he says that he is the Messiah, our king!' the Jewish leaders informed Pilate.

Pilate looked at Jesus. 'Are you the king of the Jews?' he asked him.

Jesus answered, 'You have said so.'

Pilate was sure that Jesus was innocent and did not deserve to die. However, the Jewish leaders were agitated that Pilate wanted to release Jesus. They began to shout, '**Crucify** him! Crucify him!'

'I find no guilt in him,' said Pilate, straining to be heard over the din. 'But you have a custom that I should set free a prisoner at Passover. Do you want me to release this king of the Jews?'

'No!' they yelled back. 'We want you to free Barabbas!' Barabbas was in prison for causing an uprising against the Roman authorities and for murder. Pilate gave in and ordered his soldiers to set Barabbas free.

Jesus was taken away to be beaten. The soldiers made a crown of thorns and forced it on his head. They put a purple robe on him and mocked him. 'Praise to the king of the Jews!' they shouted, and they punched him repeatedly.

When the soldiers had their fun, they took the purple robe off Jesus and put on his own clothes. Pilate presented Jesus to the Jews. 'Look! Here is your king!'

'Only Caesar is our king!' they shouted back. 'Crucify Jesus!'

Pilate gave Jesus over to them to be crucified.

## WHAT'S THE POINT:

Why was Jesus sentenced to death? Well, the Jews wanted him dead. In their pride, they refused to believe that Jesus was the Messiah. They neither knew nor feared God. Pilate was driven by fear and wanted to protect his reputation as governor. He was easily persuaded to execute Jesus. The Jews and Pilate show the natural reaction of every rebellious soul to the Lord Jesus. But crucially, Jesus was in control of the situation. He was obeying the will of his Father. His death on the cross brings salvation to all who believe in him.

## LOOK BACK:

Read Isaiah 26:13

The Jews claimed to be God's people, but their loyalties lay elsewhere.

## CHECK THIS OUT:

Read Exodus 23:7

Given the choice between pardoning the guilty Barabbas or the innocent Jesus, the Jews opted for Barabbas. They denied the character of God whose name they claimed.

## THINK:

Can you think of a good reason why Jesus would die for you?

# THE CRUCIFIXION

## From Matthew 27, Mark 15, Luke 23, & John 19

Jesus was taken away to be crucified outside the city walls. The Roman soldiers gave him a heavy wooden cross to carry. Jesus was weak from being beaten, so he stumbled under the weight of it. The soldiers grabbed a man called Simon, from Cyrene in North Africa, to carry the cross for Jesus.

They came to **Golgotha,** and there they crucified Jesus. It was only nine o'clock in the morning. They put a sign above his head which read, 'The King of the Jews.'

In agony, Jesus prayed, 'Father, forgive them. They do not know what they are doing.'

On the ground before him, the soldiers divided up his clothes. Jesus' robe was in one piece and without seams. The soldiers did not want to tear it. They decided to throw a dice to see who got it, fulfilling the Scripture that said, 'They divided my clothes among themselves and gambled for my robe.'

Two criminals were crucified on either side of Jesus. Onlookers hurled insults at Jesus. 'If you truly are the Son of God, come down from the cross!' they jeered.

The Jewish leaders scorned him and yelled at him, 'You saved others, but you cannot save yourself! 'You are the king of the Jews! Why don't you come down from the cross, and then we will believe in you!'

One of the criminals hanging there called to Jesus. 'Are you not God's Chosen One? Save yourself and save us too!'

'Be quiet!' shouted the other criminal. 'Do you not fear God? We are getting what we deserve for our crimes, but this man has done nothing wrong!' Then he spoke to Jesus. 'Remember me, Jesus, when you come into your kingdom.'

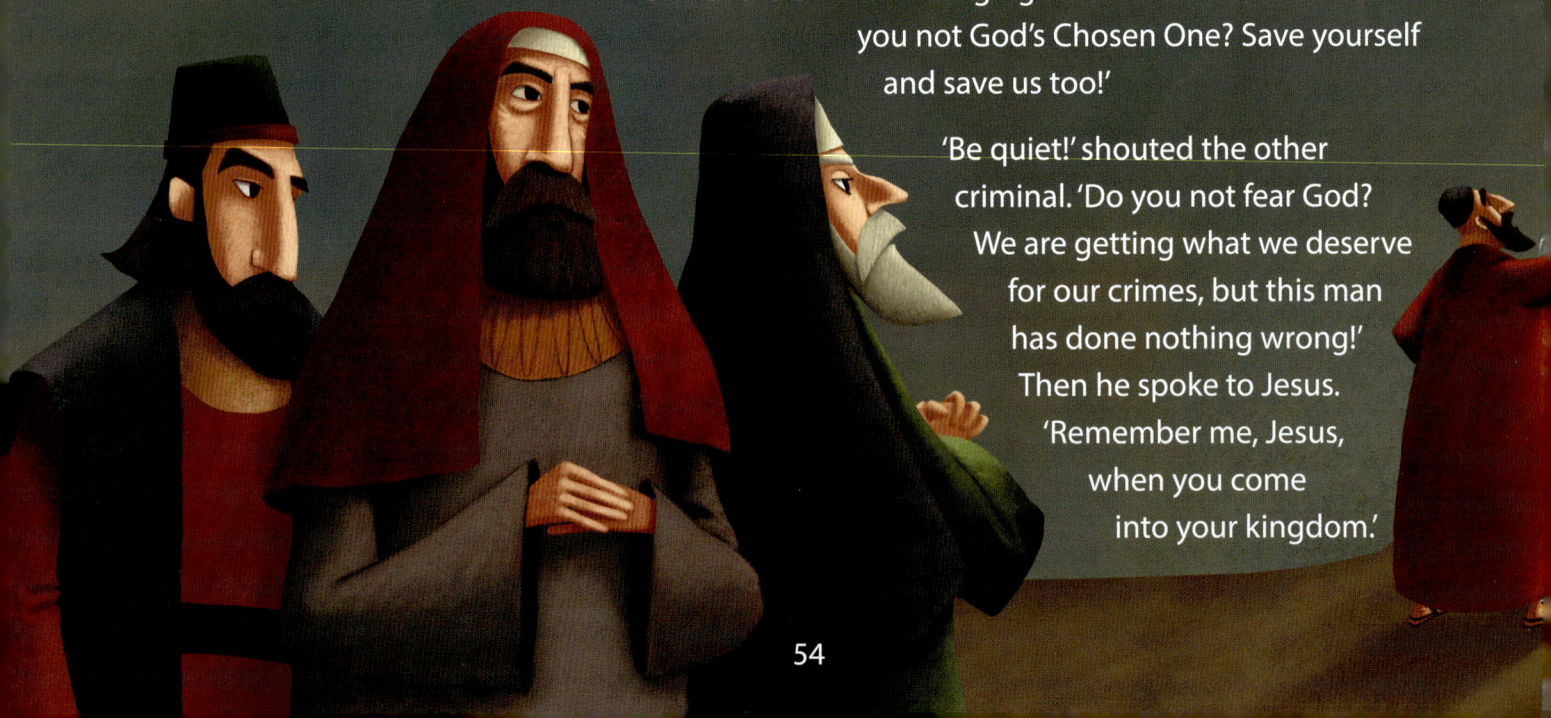

'Today you will be with me in Paradise,' Jesus promised him.

At midday, when the sun was high in the sky, darkness came over the land. It lasted for three hours. Jesus called out in a loud voice, 'My God, why have you forsaken me?'

Three hours later he said, 'I am thirsty.' They soaked a sponge in some wine vinegar and held it up to Jesus to drink.

After this, Jesus declared, 'It is finished!' And then he called out in a loud voice, 'Father into your hands I place my spirit.'

Jesus took his final breath and died.

At that moment back in Jerusalem, the temple curtain was torn in two from top to bottom. The earth quaked, rocks split, and graves were opened.

When the Roman commander and the others watching over Jesus saw the earthquake and everything else that happened, they were awestruck and declared, 'Truly this man was the Son of God!'

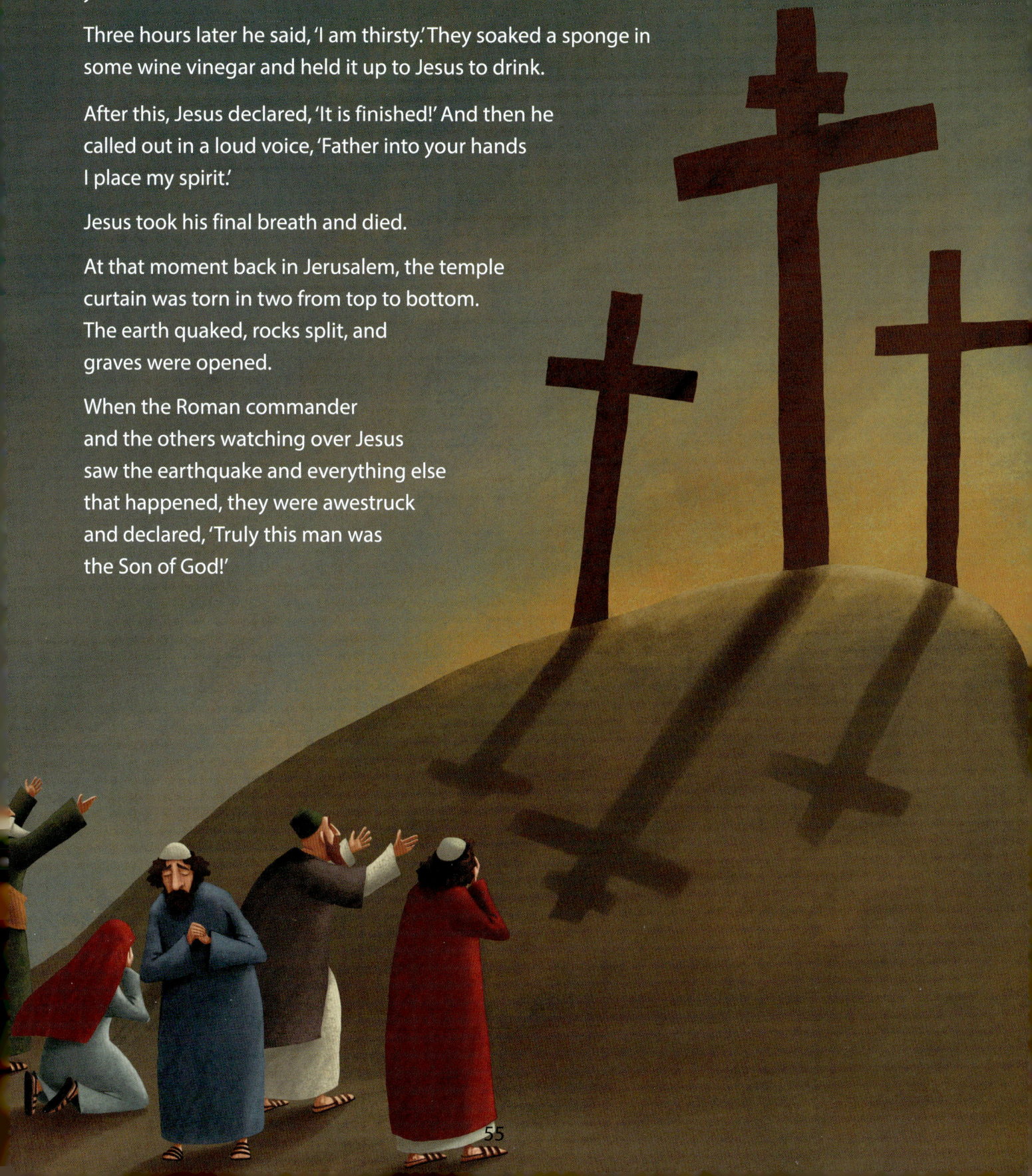

## WHAT'S THE POINT:

At the cross, Jesus endured the death he predicted for the sins of the world. God's anger at sin was poured out on Jesus. Jesus took the punishment that we deserve for our evil ways. Jesus became our **substitute**. Now we can know God's rescue, know God's forgiveness and be reconciled to him forever. We can be restored to God, come near to God without the need for priestly sacrifices in special buildings. We can know his peace.

## LOOK BACK:

Read Psalm 22:1, 7-8, 18

This psalm was fulfilled at the crucifixion of Jesus.

## CHECK THIS OUT:

Exodus 26:31-33 and Leviticus 16:2, 30

The curtain in the temple in Jerusalem separated the Holy Place from the Most Holy Place. It was like a no entry sign to God's people. Only the high priest was allowed to enter the Most Holy Place once a year on the **Day of Atonement**. On that day, he would go into God's presence and offer a sacrifice for the sins of God's people, restoring the relationship between them and God.

## LOOK FORWARD:

Hebrews 10:19-23, Romans 5:8-11 and 1 Peter 3:18

Jesus' death ended the need for priests to offer sacrifices to take away sins. There is no longer any barrier standing between God and his people. We can come near to God at any time because of Jesus' sacrifice for us. We can be accepted by God because of Jesus' sacrifice.

## CHECK THIS OUT TOO:

Read Exodus 10:21-23, Joel 2:10 and Amos 8:9-10

Darkness in the daytime was a sign of God's anger and judgement. Amos was told that a day of terrible divine judgement was coming. At the crucifixion, the darkened sky pointed to the truth that the Son of God was bearing the judgement of God.

## THINK:

Galatians 2:20 says, 'The Son of God loved me and gave himself for me.' Can you truly echo these words in your heart?

# THE RESURRECTION
## From Matthew 28, Mark 16, Luke 24 & John 20

Pontius Pilate was approached by two followers of Jesus, Joseph and Nicodemus. They wanted to bury Jesus properly and they asked Pilate to give them his body. Pilate agreed. Before Jesus was taken down from the cross, a soldier pierced his side with a spear, to make sure he was dead.

The men took Jesus' body, wrapped it in linen cloths, and covered it with many spices weighing about seventy-five pounds. This was done according to the burial custom of the Jews. They took his body to a garden where a new tomb had been cut out of the rock. It belonged to Joseph. They laid Jesus' body in the tomb and rolled a large stone over the entrance to secure it. Some of the women who were Jesus' friends, including Mary Magdalene, followed the men and saw where his body was buried. They waited for a while before returning home, as the next day was the Sabbath.

The Pharisees were worried that Jesus' followers would steal his body from the tomb and pretend that Jesus had risen from the dead. They asked Pilate for help. He provided Roman soldiers to guard the tomb where Jesus' body lay.

When the Sabbath day was over, Mary Magdalene and her friends went back to the tomb at dawn. As they approached the tomb, they saw that the stone had been rolled away from the entrance! Mary ran to get Peter and John. 'They've taken the Lord from the tomb, and we don't know where they've put him!' she exclaimed.

Peter and John ran quickly to the tomb. John got there first because he was faster than Peter. From the entrance, John peered into the tomb and saw the linen cloths lying there. Peter went into the tomb and also saw the head cloth lying separate from the linen cloths. It was neatly folded. It had been put in a different place from the rest.

They didn't understand what had happened and went back to tell the other disciples. Mary and her friends stayed behind. Mary wept bitterly.

She peered into the tomb once again and to her surprise she saw two angels sitting where Jesus' body had been.

'Why are you crying?' the angels asked her.

'They've taken my Lord away, and I don't know where they've put him,' she replied.

She turned around and saw a man approaching her. The man asked Mary, 'Why are you weeping? Who are you looking for?'

Thinking he was the gardener, Mary said, 'Sir, if you have taken his body away, tell me where, and I will take him back.'

'Mary,' said Jesus gently.

Mary recognised that voice! She had heard Jesus say it so many times in exactly the same way!

'Master!' she cried out.

'Go and tell my brothers that I have risen,' Jesus told her. 'Say to them, "I am going to my Father, who is also your Father." And tell them to go to Galilee. They will see me there.'

Overjoyed that they had seen the risen Lord Jesus, Mary and her friends ran quickly from the garden, to tell the disciples that Jesus is alive!

## WHAT'S THE POINT:

Jesus truly died and his body was missing from the tomb. It wasn't stolen. Jesus' body passed through the linen cloths that had been weighed down by all the spices. The linen cloths lay where his body had been placed. It was a physical resurrection. It was a miracle! This means Jesus is Lord of life and death. There is no greater love than his love for us, and no greater hope than the certain hope he gives us that our sins are forgiven, and we can have eternal life with him in heaven.

## LOOK FORWARD:

Read 1 Corinthians 15:20-22, 54-57

Death is the enemy. The resurrection of Jesus, however, means that death is no longer to be feared by those who trust in him. Death has been defeated by Jesus.

## CHECK THIS OUT:

Read Acts 17:30-31

The resurrection of Jesus Christ from the dead is proof that Judgement Day is coming. God calls on everyone, everywhere, to repent and turn back to him before it does.

## THINK:

Jesus is risen from the dead. He is the King of kings and Lord of lords. Does he sit on the throne of your life?

# SEEING IS BELIEVING

## From Luke 24 and John 20-21

The disciples kept the doors locked because they were afraid that the Jews might come after them next. Thomas was not with them.

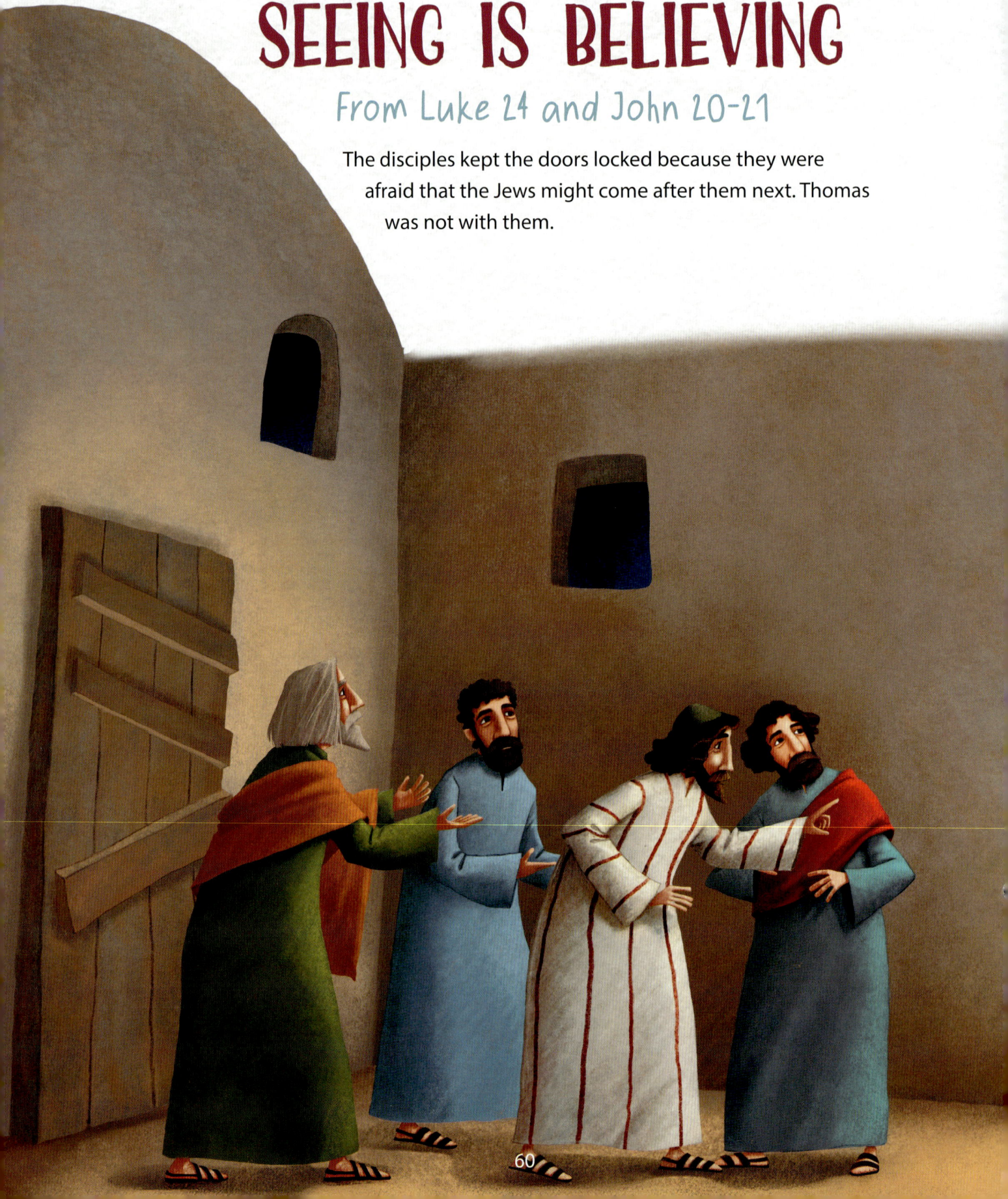

Suddenly Jesus stood among the disciples! They were even more frightened because they thought he was a ghost.

Jesus greeted them. 'Peace be with you. Look at my hands and my feet. Go ahead, touch me. See for yourselves that I am not a ghost,' Jesus said as he held out his hands.

The disciples' fear turned to joy at seeing the Lord.

Jesus asked them, 'Have you got anything to eat here?' They gave him some cooked fish and he ate it in front of them.

When he had finished eating, he said, 'Remember when I was with you, I told you everything that was written about me in the Law of Moses, in the writings of the prophets and in the Psalms had to be fulfilled.'

At that moment Jesus opened their minds so they could understand the Scriptures. 'This is what is written,' he began. 'It was necessary for the Christ to suffer and rise from the dead on the third day. And now, in Christ's name, the good news of repentance and forgiveness of sins must be preached to every nation, starting at Jerusalem. You are all witnesses of these things. I will send you the one my Father promised. In the meantime, wait in Jerusalem until you receive power from heaven.'

Thomas did not arrive until after Jesus left the disciples.

'We have seen the Lord!' they told him excitedly.

'Really? Well, unless I see the nail marks in his hands and touch the scar in his side, I'll never believe you!' he replied sceptically.

A week later, the disciples were inside together, and the doors were locked. This time, Thomas was there. Suddenly Jesus stood among them and greeted them. 'Peace be with you,' he said. Then he looked at Thomas and said, 'Stick your finger here and look at my hands. Stretch out your hand and touch my side. Stop doubting, Thomas, and believe!'

Then Thomas declared, 'My Lord and my God!'

'Do you believe because you have seen me, Thomas? How blessed are those who believe in me without seeing me!' said Jesus.

## WHAT'S THE POINT:

The disciples were doubtful that anyone could rise from the dead. They needed evidence of the resurrection, or they would not believe it. Jesus addressed their doubting hearts and minds by appealing to their senses – touch and sight. Jesus showed them his scars. He ate fish. They saw that his resurrection was physical. Jesus opened their minds to the Word of God, which must be the foundation of faith and life in him.

The gospel of Christ had to be their message. It had to be preached in the power of the Holy Spirit, to help others come to know the Lord Jesus. It is the Holy Spirit who enables us to become children of God.

## LOOK BACK:

Read Micah 7:18-19 and Psalm 79:8-9

God is full of grace and mercy to his sinful people. His name is glorified in the act of forgiving sinners. Jesus is Immanuel – 'God with us.' How does Jesus treat those who deserted him?

## CHECK THIS OUT:

Read John 20:1-29

The disciples didn't expect Jesus to rise from the dead, even though he told them he would. It was what they saw that changed their minds. How many times is the 'seeing' word used in this passage?

## THINK:

The first disciples saw the risen Jesus and believed. Do you believe their testimony? If so, how will it change your life?

# JESUS AND PETER

## From John 21

One evening Peter went fishing with John and some other disciples on the western side of the Sea of Galilee. They worked through the night but did not catch any fish.

Jesus was standing on the shore as the sun was coming up. The disciples did not recognise him. Jesus called to them. 'My friends, did you catch any fish?'

'No!' came the reply from the boat.

'Throw your net over the right side of the boat. You'll catch some there,' Jesus said.

As soon as the men tossed the net over the right side of the boat, it filled up with fish! They could hardly pull the net into the boat because the catch was so heavy.

'That's Jesus!' exclaimed John to Peter. Immediately Peter threw himself into the water and swam to the shore. The other disciples sailed behind him, dragging the net full of fish in the water, because they were only a short distance from the shore.

By the time they got to shore, Jesus had already started a fire and was cooking some fish that he had. There was bread as well.

Jesus said to them, 'Get some more fish from your haul.' Peter went to the boat and got some. The men had counted one hundred and fifty-three fish in total. It was a super catch, and it didn't even damage the nets.

'Come and eat some breakfast,' Jesus said to his disciples. None of the disciples dared ask him who he was. They all knew it was the Lord Jesus.

After they had eaten, Jesus walked along the shore with Peter. Jesus asked Peter the same question three times: 'Do you love me?'

Peter was sorrowful, remembering how he rejected knowing Jesus three times. He answered, 'Lord, you know all things. You know that I love you.'

'Well then, look after my sheep.' Jesus commanded Peter. Jesus had forgiven Peter.

'Follow me, Peter,' said Jesus, and Peter obeyed.

## WHAT'S THE POINT:

Peter knew he had let the Lord down, and he felt terrible about it. Jesus forgave him, and restored him as a disciple. Jesus knew that Peter was truly sorry. Then Jesus gave Peter a vital job to do. He was commanded to look after Jesus' followers. Peter would do this by teaching them God's Word and living a holy life to please God. Anyone, no matter their past failure, can be forgiven and used in the service of Jesus Christ.

## THINK:

Are you a forgiven sinner in the service of Jesus Christ? If not, why not?

# UP AND AWAY

## From Matthew 28 and Luke 24

During the forty days after his resurrection, Jesus appeared to his disciples many times, proving to them that he was truly alive, and teaching them more about the kingdom of God.

On his last day on earth, Jesus walked with them to the Mount of Olives.

'My Father has given me all authority in heaven and on earth,' Jesus told them. 'Therefore, go to all people, all over the world and make them my disciples. Baptise them in the name of the Father, and the Son, and the Holy Spirit. Teach them to obey everything that I have commanded you. Be assured, I will always be with you, until the end of time.'

Jesus lifted up his hands to bless them. As he was blessing them, he was taken up into heaven before their eyes. Then he was gone.

The disciples went back to Jerusalem, full of joy. Every day they went to the temple and gave thanks to God for Jesus!

## WHAT'S THE POINT:

Jesus gave his disciples an important mission – to make more disciples of Jesus. The disciples were told to preach the gospel and nurture new believers with the Word of God, so that they would obey the Lord Jesus Christ. Jesus' promise to be with his disciples until the end of time means the mission is for every generation. All disciples of Jesus should use their gifts to make more disciples of Jesus. This is the only mission of his Church.

## LOOK BACK:

Read Daniel 7:9-15

Daniel's vision of the heavenly court sees the risen and ascended Lord Jesus who has all authority in heaven and on earth.

## LOOK FORWARD:

Read 1 Corinthians 15:6

Jesus appeared to over five hundred people during the forty days after his resurrection. They were all eyewitnesses to the truth that Jesus is alive!

## CHECK THIS OUT:

Read Mark 8:35 and John 17:6-26

The Lord Jesus prayed for his disciples. He wants all his disciples to live for him and his gospel. Be serious about making disciples of Jesus, even when your culture is hostile to the truth of God's Word. Remember, Jesus is always with you!

## THINK:

Are you a disciple-making disciple? If not, it's time to start!

# WHAT DOES IT MEAN?

**Atone/Day of Atonement** – to make up for a wrong act in order to fully restore a relationship. The Day of Atonement was a day once a year when sin was atoned for through animal sacrifice by the high priest, thus restoring the relationship between God and his people.

**Crucify/Crucifixion** – a form of torture where a person is nailed to a wooden cross.

**Denarius/Denarii** – a small silver coin in Roman money. A day's wages.

**Famine** – when there is not enough food to keep people and animals alive.

**Golgotha** – means 'The Place of a Skull.' It was where Jesus was crucified.

**Idol** – a statue or image of a false god. Anything that takes the place of God In a person's life.

**Levite** – a man from the tribe of Levi. Levites were responsible for the tabernacle and the temple of God. The priests were from the tribe of Levi.

**Prostitute** – someone who gets paid for having sexual relations with another person.

**Ransom** – a price required to deliver or set someone free from slavery or imprisonment.

**Reconcile** – to bring together. In the New Testament, it means to restore the relationship between God and people.

**Samaritan** – a person who lived in or came from the city of Samaria in Israel.

**Substitute** – to take the place of someone or something

**Symbolic** – using an object or an action to represent something else

**Tithe** – meaning tenth. In the Old Testament, one tenth of what you earned was given back to God.

**Transfigure** – to change in appearance or form.

# CHRISTIAN FOCUS FOR KIDS

CF4KIDS

That means you and your friends can all find a book to help you from the CF4KIDS range – from the very littlest baby to kids that are almost too old to be called a kid anymore.

We publish books that introduce you to the real Jesus, the truth of God's Word, and what that means for boys and girls of all ages.

Reading books is a fun way to find out what it is like to be a follower of Jesus Christ.

True stories, adventures, activity books, and devotions – they are all here for you and your family.

Christian Focus is part of the family of God. We aim to glorify Jesus and help you trust and follow Him.

Christian Focus Publications Ltd,

Geanies House, Fearn, Ross-shire,

IV20 1TW, Scotland,
United Kingdom.

Find us at our web page:
christianfocus.com